583
Pre

Prevost, John F.
Walnut trees

| | DATE DUE | | |
|---|---|---|---|
| | | | |
| | | | |
| | | | |
| | | | |
| | | | |
| | | | |
| | | | |
| | | | |
| | | | |
| | | | |
| | | | |

# TREES

# WALNUT TREES

John F. Prevost
ABDO & Daughters

Published by Abdo & Daughters, 4940 Viking Drive, Suite 622, Edina, Minnesota 55435.

Printed in the United States.

Cover Photo credits: Peter Arnold, Inc.
Interior Photo credits: Peter Arnold, Inc.

Edited by Bob Italia

**Library of Congress Cataloging-in-Publication Data**

Prevost, John F.
    Walnut Trees / John F. Prevost.
        p.  cm. -- (Trees)
    Includes index.
    Summary: Presents brief information about the roots, trunk, leaves, seeds, and varieties of the walnut tree, pests that affect it, its economic uses, and more.
        ISBN 1-56239-618-8
    1. Walnut--Juvenile literature.  [1. Redwood.  2. Trees.]  I. Title. II. Series: Prevost, John F. Trees.
    QK495.J85P76 1996                                                        96-309
    583'.973--dc20                                                            CIP
                                                                             AC

**ABOUT THE AUTHOR**
John Prevost is a marine biologist and diver who has been active in conservation and education issues for the past 18 years.  Currently he is living inland and remains actively involved in freshwater and marine husbandry, conservation and education projects.

# Contents

# Walnut Trees and Family

Walnut trees are large. Some may grow over 100 feet (30 meters) tall. One measured tree was over 150 feet (45 meters) tall.

Walnut trees shed their leaves in the fall. They grow slowly from seeds or **cuttings**.

Walnut trees are grown for their lumber, nuts, and beauty. They are also planted as shade trees. There are about 20 kinds of walnut trees found worldwide.

*The largest walnut trees are over 100 feet (30 meters) tall.*

# Roots, Soil, and Water

Walnut trees pull water from the ground with their deep **taproot**. This main root runs straight down from the trunk.  The other roots branch from it.

The taproot holds the tree in place.  Walnut trees are rarely damaged by high winds. But they are hard to **transplant.**  The taproot is easily damaged and the tree will die.

Walnut trees grow best in moist, rich soil. Water holds **minerals** and other **nutrients** which the trees use for food. Without enough food, the walnut trees will not grow or produce nuts.

*Walnuts being harvested.*

# Stems, Leaves, and Sunlight

Walnut trees grow well in sunny locations. Without enough sun, trees will become weak and die.

Walnut trees use sunlight to change water, **nutrients**, and air into food and **oxygen**. This process is called **photosynthesis**.

The trunk, branches and stems connect the leaves to the roots. This allows water and nutrients to reach the leaves. Food made by the leaves then travels back to the roots.

The trunk and branches are protected by a thick, wrinkled layer of **bark.** This keeps insects and other animals from damaging the tree. It also protects the walnut tree from the burning sun.

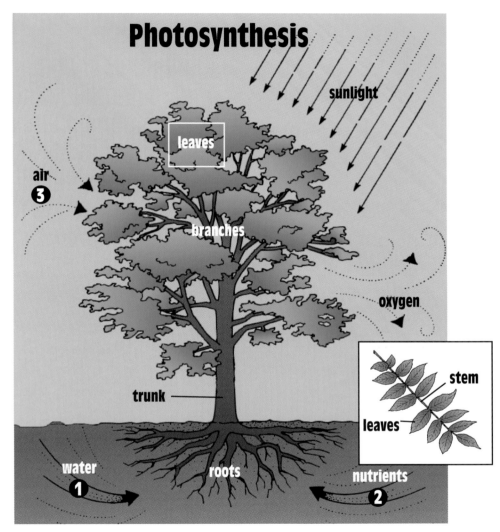

Ground water (1) and nutrients (2) travel through the roots, trunk, and branches and into the leaves where air (3) is drawn in. Then the tree uses sunlight to change these three elements into food and oxygen.

# Flowers and Seeds

Walnut trees **bloom** in the early spring. Their flowers are called **catkins.** Catkins are a long group of small, fuzzy **blossoms** that droop slightly from their stem. The male flowers are found on year-old stems. The female flowers are found on newer stems, and produce walnuts.

Walnuts grow inside thick, round **husks.** People, deer, bear, and squirrels like to eat walnuts. A stain can be made from the husks and is used on wood, leather, and paper.

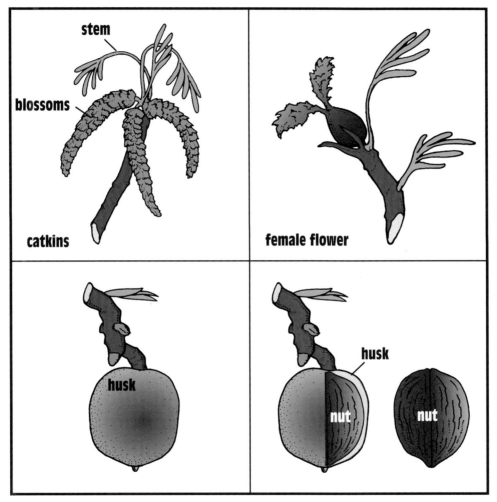

stem

blossoms

catkins

female flower

husk

husk

nut

nut

*Some catkins grow female flowers which produce walnuts.*
*A protective husk grows around each walnut.*

# Insects and Other Friends

Walnut trees are home to several hundred insects and mites. Many are **pollinators** and **predators** that control **pests.**

Many birds and small **mammals** nest in walnut trees. They feed their young on pests. Others use the tree for shelter but eat pests elsewhere. Squirrels, chipmunks, and bats are often found in or around walnut trees.

*Many mammals enjoy the fruit of the walnut tree.*

# Pests and Diseases

**Aphids**, webworm, and codling moth are the main walnut tree **pests. Predatory** insects such as wasps can control these pests. Insect sprays also work.

**Diseases** can attack walnut trees weakened by pests or other injury. Insects may also spread diseases as they feed. **Chemicals** are used to control diseases.

*Predatory insects such as wasps feed on insect pests.*

*Squirrels and blue jays eat the nuts of the walnut tree.*

15

# Varieties

There are four types of walnut trees grown in North America: butternut, black walnut, California black walnut, and Persian (English) walnut.

The butternut is found the farthest north, into Canada. The black walnut is not found as far north. In the United States, most Persian walnuts grow in the West, Midwest, and Northeast. The California black walnut is found mostly in California.

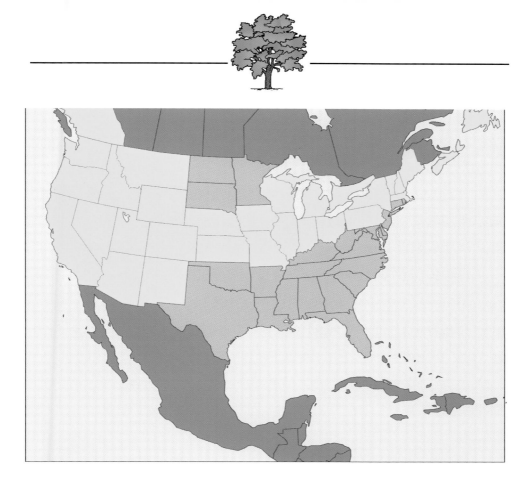

**In North America, most Persian walnut trees are grown in the West, Midwest, and Northeast (yellow). Their nuts are a popular snack food.**

# Uses

Walnut trees are grown for their nuts and wood. The nuts are used in baked goods, candy, and to make cooking oil. People buy the Persian walnut as a snack food. Black walnuts are also popular but have a stronger taste.

Walnut tree wood is used in furniture. It is one of the finest-looking woods.

*Opposite page:*
*The beginning stages of*
*the walnut and its fruit.*

# Walnut Trees and the Plant Kingdom

The plant kingdom is divided into several groups, including flowering plants, fungi, plants with bare seeds, and ferns.

 Flowering plants grow flowers to make seeds. These seeds often grow inside protective ovaries or fruit.

 Fungi are plants without leaves, flowers, or green coloring, and cannot make their own food. They include mushrooms, molds, and yeast.

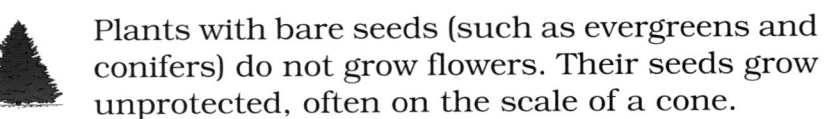 Plants with bare seeds (such as evergreens and conifers) do not grow flowers. Their seeds grow unprotected, often on the scale of a cone.

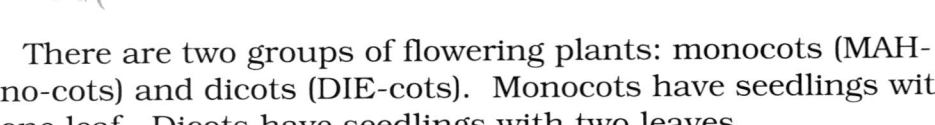 Ferns are plants with roots, stems, and leaves. They do not grow flowers or seeds.

There are two groups of flowering plants: monocots (MAH-no-cots) and dicots (DIE-cots). Monocots have seedlings with one leaf. Dicots have seedlings with two leaves.

The walnut family is one type of dicot.

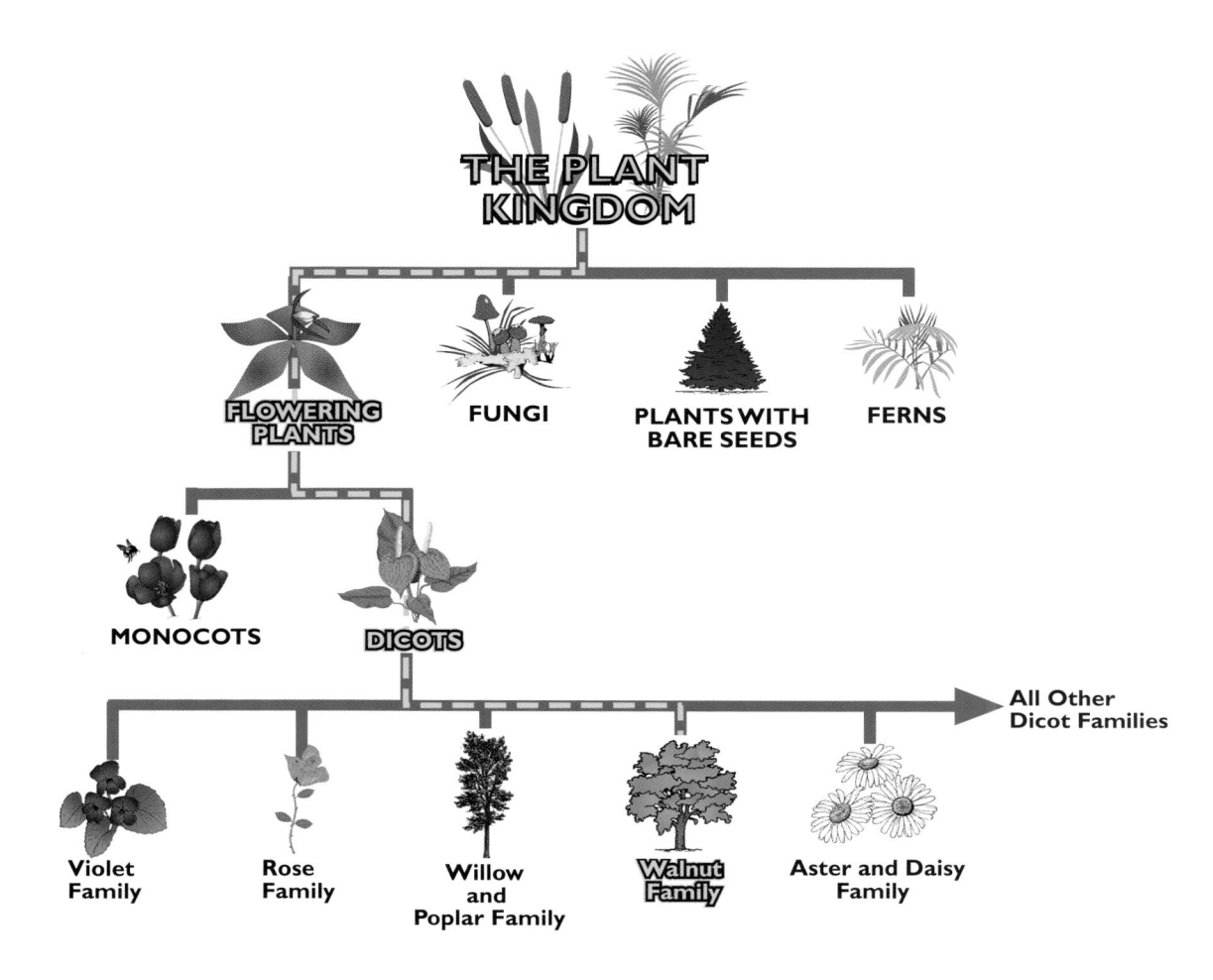

THE PLANT KINGDOM

FLOWERING PLANTS

FUNGI

PLANTS WITH BARE SEEDS

FERNS

MONOCOTS

DICOTS

All Other Dicot Families

Violet Family

Rose Family

Willow and Poplar Family

Walnut Family

Aster and Daisy Family

# Glossary

**aphid** (AY-fid) - A small insect that sucks the sap from plant leaves and stems.

**bark** - The tough outside covering of the trunk and branches of trees.

**bloom** - To have flowers; a flower blossom.

**blossom** (BLAH-sum) - The flower of a plant.

**catkin** - The cluster of flowers found on birches, oaks, and willows.

**chemical** (KEM-ih-kull) - A substance used to create a reaction or process.

**cutting** - A bud or stem of a plant that is used to start a new plant.

**deciduous** (dah-SID-you-us) - Trees which lose their leaves in the fall.

**disease** (diz-EEZ) - A sickness.

**husk** - The thick skin surrounding the walnut.

**mammal** - A class of animals, including humans, that have hair and feed their young milk.

**mineral** (MIN-er-ull) - Any substance that is not a plant, animal, or another living thing.

**nutrient** (NEW-tree-ent) - Substance that promotes growth or good health.

**oxygen** (OX-ih-gen) - A gas without color, taste, or odor found in air and water.

**pest** - A harmful or destructive insect.

**photosynthesis** (foe-toe-SIN-thuh-sis) - Producing food using sunlight as the source of energy.

**pollinate** (PAH-lin-ate) - To move pollen from flower to flower, allowing them to develop seeds.

**predator** (PRED-uh-tore) - An animal that eats other animals.

**shelterbelt** - A group of trees protecting buildings or fields from wind and other weather.

**taproot** - A main root of a plant with smaller roots coming off its sides.

**transplant** - To move a plant by digging it up and moving it with the surrounding soil.

**veneer** - A thin layer of wood used to decorate or protect a surface.

# Index